Contents

Introduction

Oxford Reading Tree stories at Stages 5 to 9 continue to feature the familiar characters from previous stages in stories that reflect the experiences of most children. The magic key, discovered at Stage 4, also takes children into exciting fantasy adventures, widening and enriching their reading experience.

The stories still use natural language, phonically decodable words and high frequency words, all illustrated with funny and engaging pictures. Reading them will enable children to practise different reading skills, and continue to develop their word recognition and language comprehension.

Using the books

This booklet provides suggestions for using the books for guided, group and independent activities. The reading activities include ideas for developing children's *word recognition* W and *language comprehension* C skills. Within word recognition, there are ideas for helping children practise their phonic skills and knowledge, as well as helping them to tackle words that are not easy to decode phonically. The language comprehension ideas include suggestions for teaching the skills of prediction, questioning, clarifying, summarising and imagining in order to help children understand the text and the whole stories. Suggestions are also provided for speaking, listening, drama and writing activities.

Reading fluency

To support children in developing fluency in their reading, give them plenty of opportunities to revisit the stories. This includes:

- rereading independently
- rereading with a partner
- rereading at home

- listening to audio versions of the story (e.g. Talking Stories)
- hearing the story read to them by others as they follow the printed text.

Rereading and rehearing helps children develop automatic word recognition and gives them models of fluent, expressive reading.

Comprehension strategies

Story	Comprehension strategy taught through these Teaching Notes				
	Prediction	Questioning	Clarifying	Summarising	Imagining
The Kidnappers	✓	✓	✓	✓	✓
Viking Adventure	✓	✓	✓	✓	✓
The Rainbow Machine	✓	✓	✓	✓	✓
The Flying Carpet	✓	✓	✓	✓	✓
A Day in London	✓	✓	✓	✓	✓
Victorian Adventure	✓	✓	✓	✓	✓

Vocabulary and phonic opportunities

Each story contains many decodable words, providing lots of opportunities to practice phonic and word recognition skills. The chart shows the tricky words used in each book. The tricky words are common but do not conform to the phonic rules taught up to this point – children will need support to learn and recognise them. If children struggle with one of these words you can model how to read it.

The Kidnappers	Tricky words	after, another, beautiful, because, busy, could, course, everyone, friends, laughed, lose, many, read, sign, something, through, trouble, wanted, what, working, would
Viking Adventure	Tricky words	after, because, beautiful, before, being, cold, could, door, either, fierce, frightened, idea, school, through, told, wanted, work, wonder
The Rainbow Machine	Tricky words	again, any, because, before, changed, double, field, heavy, move, other, people, ready, straight, though, thought, young, want, where, worked, worry
The Flying Carpet	Tricky words	after, again, already, beautiful, because, before, believe, coming, doesn't, instead, kind, learning, people, school, someone, son, thought, through, want, wonder, worth, where, your
A Day in London	Tricky words	after, again, another, because, bought, brought, comes, everyone, famous, fierce, heights, instead, money, noise, people, scene, sight, trouble, where, worse
Victorian Adventure	Tricky words	bought, bread, friends, great, heads, important, school, shoe, shouldn't, station, taught, together, tonight, towards, trouble, where, work, wouldn't, your

Curriculum coverage chart

	Speaking, listening, drama	Reading	Writing
The Kidnappers			
PNS Literacy Framework (Y2)	1.3	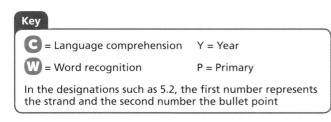 **W** 5.1, 5.3, 5.5 **C** 7.4, 7.5, 8.3	9.4
National Curriculum	Working towards Level 2		
Scotland (5–14)	Level A/B	Level A/B	Level A/B
N. Ireland (P3/Y3)	1, 2, 5, 8, 10, 11	1, 3, 4, 5, 11, 14, 15	1, 2, 3, 5, 6, 10, 11, 12, 13
Wales (Key Stage 1)	Range: 1, 3, 5 Skills: 1, 3	Range: 2, 4, 5, 6 Skills: 1, 2	Range: 3, 7 Skills: 1, 5, 7, 8
Viking Adventure			
PNS Literacy Framework (Y2)	4.1	**W** 5.1, 5.3, 5.4, 5.5 **C** 7.1, 7.4, 8.3	11.2
National Curriculum	Working towards Level 2		
Scotland (5–14)	Level A/B	Level A/B	Level A/B
N. Ireland (P3/Y3)	1, 2, 5, 6, 7, 10, 11	1, 3, 4, 8, 11, 14	1, 2, 3, 5, 10, 11, 12, 13
Wales (Key Stage 1)	Range: 1, 2, 5 Skills: 3, 4	Range: 2, 4, 5, 6 Skills: 1, 2	Range: 3 Skills: 6 Language development: 1

Key

C = Language comprehension   Y = Year

W = Word recognition   P = Primary

In the designations such as 5.2, the first number represents the strand and the second number the bullet point

Curriculum coverage chart

	Speaking, listening, drama	Reading	Writing
The Rainbow Machine			
PNS Literacy Framework (Y2)	4.1	Ⓦ 5.1, 5.3, 5.5 Ⓒ 7.4, 7.5, 8.3	9.1
National Curriculum	Working within level 2		
Scotland (5–14)	Level A/B	Level A/B	Level A/B
N. Ireland (P3/Y3)	1, 2, 5, 6, 10, 11, 13	1, 3, 4, 5, 11, 15, 16	1, 2, 3, 5, 7, 8, 10, 11, 12, 13
Wales (Key Stage 1)	Range: 1, 2, 5 Skills: 3, 4	Range: 2, 4, 5, 6 Skills: 1, 2	Range: 3, 4, 5 Skills: 5, 7, 8
The Flying Carpet			
PNS Literacy Framework (Y2)	4.2	Ⓦ 5.1, 5.2, 5.3, 5.5 Ⓒ 7,1, 7.4	8.3
National Curriculum	Working within level 2		
Scotland (5–14)	Level A/B	Level A/B	Level A/B
N. Ireland (P3/Y3)	1, 2, 5, 6, 7, 9, 10, 11	1, 3, 4, 5, 11, 12, 16, 17	1, 2, 3, 5, 7, 8, 10, 11, 12, 13
Wales (Key Stage 1)	Range: 1, 2, 5 Skills: 1, 2, 4	Range: 2, 4, 5, 6 Skills: 1, 2	Range: 3, 6 Skills: 5, 7, 8

Curriculum coverage chart

	Speaking, listening, drama	Reading	Writing
A Day in London			
PNS Literacy Framework (Y2)	4.1	**W** 5.1, 5.3, 5.5 **C** 7.1, 7.4, 7.5	9.1
National Curriculum	Working within level 2		
Scotland (5–14)	Level A/B	Level A/B	Level A/B
N. Ireland (P3/Y3)	1, 2, 5, 6, 7, 8, 10, 11	1, 3, 4, 5, 8, 15, 16	1, 2, 3, 5, 10, 11, 12, 15
Wales (Key Stage 1)	Range: 1, 2, 3, 5 Skills:1, 3, 4	Range: 2, 4, 5, 6 Skills: 1, 2	Range: 3, 6 Skills: 5, 7, 8
Victorian Adventure			
PNS Literacy Framework (Y2)	1.3	**W** 5.1, 5.2, 5.3, 5.5 **C** 7.1, 7.2, 7.4, 8.3	9.1
National Curriculum	1a, f	1a, d, f, g, j, l, n, 3b, 6a	1b, c, d, 2a,b
Scotland (5–14)	Level A/B	Level A/B	Level A/B
N. Ireland (P3/Y3))	1, 2, 5, 6, 7, 8, 10, 11	1, 3, 4, 5, 8, 11, 12, 17	1, 2, 3, 5, 7, 8, 10, 11, 12, 13
Wales (Key Stage 1)	Range: 1, 2, 5 Skills: 1, 2, 3	Range: 2, 4, 5, 6 Skills: 1, 2	Range: 3, 6 Skills: 4, 5, 7, 8

The Kidnappers

> **C** = Language comprehension   *R, AF* = QCA reading assessment focus
>
> **W** = Word recognition   *W, AF* = QCA writing assessment focus

Group or guided reading

Introducing the book

C *(Clarifying)* Read the title and have a quick look through the pictures. Ask: *What do kidnappers do? Who do they kidnap and why?*

C *(Questioning)* Ask: *What do you notice about the characters on the cover? Which famous character is being kidnapped? How do you know?*

C *(Prediction)* Read the blurb on the back cover. Look through some of the pictures and ask the children to suggest why the magic changes Kipper into a teddy bear.

Strategy check

Remind the children to use syllables when reading longer words (e.g. 'Swit–zer–land' on page 7).

Independent reading

● Ask children to read the story. Remind them to use phonics and the sense of the sentence to work out new words. Praise children for reading silently with concentration.

C *(Prediction)* If appropriate, pause at page 19 or page 23 and ask the child to say what will happen next.

Assessment Check that children:

● *(R, AF1)* read independently and with increasing fluency longer and less familiar texts

● *(R, AF1)* know how to tackle words that are not completely decodable (see chart on page 4)

● *(R, AF1)* read high and medium frequency words independently and automatically

- (R, AF1) use syntax and context to build their store of vocabulary when reading for meaning.

Returning to the text

C (*Summarising*) Ask children to explain how Kipper and his friends rescued the famous bears from the kidnappers.

C (*Questioning*) Ask them to think of questions they would like to ask Kipper about his adventure.

C (*Questioning*) Look at page 19, ask: *How does Bunbury know it is a kidnapping?*

C (*Questioning*) Ask: *How and why does Kipper's appearance change for this adventure?*

C (*Imagining*) Ask: *What do you think might have happened to the famous bears if Kipper hadn't rescued them?*

Group and independent reading activities

Objective Know how to tackle words that are not completely decodable (5.3).

W On page 9, ask children to find 'beautiful'. Ask: *If you didn't know this word, how could you work it out?* Talk about the parts that are easy to decode: ('b'....'tiful'), then read the whole sentence and ask the children to suggest words that would fit. Match a suggestion with the decoded parts of the word and read 'beautiful'.

Assessment (R, AF1) Can the children show you how to read 'sign' on page 18 in the same way?

Objective Read high and medium frequency words independently and automatically (5.5).

W Using some of the words listed for this story on page 4, play flashcard games where children practise reading the words quickly in any order. Focus on 'because'. Ask the children to find 'because' on page 27. Ask questions that need 'because' in the answer, e.g. *Why did the plane go to Switzerland? Why was Catsimir driving the honey van? Why did the famous bears climb out of a window?* Write the children's answer to each question on the board, then read the sentences together.

Assessment (R, AF1) Can children read high frequency words quickly and confidently? Did they read 'because' on sight?

Objective Explore how particular words are used, including words with similar meanings (7.5).

● Read the first three sentences on page 19. Ask the children if they can think of other words that could be used instead of 'famous', 'trouble' and 'nasty'. (Ideas could include: 'well known', 'popular', 'celebrity'; 'a problem', 'a fuss', 'a worry'; 'unpleasant', 'mean', 'unkind'.) Use the children's ideas, in turn, in the sentences. Read the whole sentence each time you replace a word to find out if it sounds right. You can also use a dictionary or thesaurus for more ideas. Decide which words best retain the meaning of the story.

Assessment (R, AF1) Can the children think of alternative words for 'sped' and 'saw' on page 20? Do the words fit the context and retain the meaning?

Objective Explain their reactions to texts, commenting on important aspects (8.3).

C (Clarifying) Read page 32 together. Look at the picture. Ask the children to explain whether Kipper had an adventure or a dream. Ask: *What makes you think that? Why didn't Biff and Chip believe him? Is there any proof?* (Ask the children to look in the picture to see what Kipper brought back from the adventure, i.e. the honey pot!)

Assessment (R, AF3) Can children explain their deductions and give evidence for them?

Speaking, listening and drama activities

Objective Explain ideas using imaginative and adventurous vocabulary and non-verbal gestures to support communication (1.3).

● Read page 32 together. Ask three children to be in the hot seat as Biff, Chip and Kipper. The rest of the group or class ask the characters questions, e.g. *Why do Biff and Chip think Kipper's adventure was a dream? Why was Kipper so sure that it was a magic adventure? Can Kipper prove it was a magic adventure? Would Kipper have remembered such a detailed dream? Why did the key glow when it hadn't glowed for a long time?*

- When lots of questions have been asked and answered, let the group vote on whether Kipper had an adventure or a dream.

Assessment *(R, AF3)* Can children infer what has happened to Kipper from the events and information in the story and pictures?

Writing activities

Objective Make adventurous word and language choices appropriate to the style and purpose of the text (9.4).

- Ask the children to read pages 26 and 27 again. Talk about words that would make the escape sound dangerous and exciting. Make a list of useful words and phrases, such as 'silently', 'nervously', 'as fast as they could', 'their hearts in their mouths', 'anxiously', 'hearts thumping', 'afraid of being seen'.

- Ask the children to rewrite these two pages independently, showing how everyone was terrified of the nasty bears.

Assessment *(R, AF7)* Ask the children to read their work aloud. Does the sense of excitement and danger come across? Ask them to tell you the words and phrases that achieve this.

Viking Adventure

> **C** = Language comprehension   *R, AF* = QCA reading assessment focus
>
> **W** = Word recognition   *W, AF* = QCA writing assessment focus

Group or guided reading

Introducing the book

- Read the title and have a quick look through the pictures to see what happens.

C *(Prediction)* Ask: *What do you think the story is about? What do you think will happen in the story?*

C *(Clarifying)* Ask: *What do you know about the Vikings?* If necessary, explain that 'Vikings' is the name given to sea-faring people from Denmark, Sweden and Norway who lived over a thousand years ago. Look at their ships, helmets and shields in the pictures.

Strategy check

Remind the children to reread a sentence if it does not seem to make sense.

Independent reading

- Ask the children to read the story. Encourage them to tackle unfamiliar words by using syllables, phonics and the sense of the sentence. Praise and encourage fluent expressive reading when they read aloud to you.

Assessment Check that children:

- *(R, AF1)* read independently with increasing fluency longer and less familiar texts (5.1)

- *(R, AF1)* know how to tackle unfamiliar words (5.3)

- *(R, AF1)* use syntax and context to build their store of vocabulary when reading for meaning (7.4).

Returning to the text

 (Questioning, Clarifying) Go to page 7. Ask: *Would you agree with Biff that it was hard work being a Viking?* Ask the children to use the text to give reasons for their answers.

 (Summarising, Questioning) Ask: *What did you find out about the way the Vikings lived from reading this story? What did they wear? What did they eat? Where did they live? How did they travel? Why did they need helmets and shields?* Ask the children to tell you the page numbers that provide the answers. Ask everyone to find the page number each time and read the sentence that gives the answer.

Group and independent reading activities

Objective Read high and medium frequency words independently and automatically (5.5).

 Ask the children to take turns to read aloud a few pages each of the story. Praise them for confident reading. Choose high frequency words from the list on page 4 and write them on separate pieces of card. Place the cards face down on the table. Ask the children to turn over a card and read the word. Praise children for recognising the words on sight.

Assessment *(R, AF1)* Do the children read confidently? Note any words that cause them to hesitate.

Objective Draw together ideas and information from across a whole text (7.1).

 (Questioning, Imagining) On page 21, ask children to imagine that they are the Viking children seeing sweets for the first time. What questions would they want to ask Kipper? Turn to page 22 and ask children to imagine being Biff, Chip, Wilf and Kipper. Ask: *What questions would you want to ask the Vikings about their home?* Look at page 23. Ask: *How comfortable do you think it was to sleep here? How would you keep warm? Do you think it would be easy to cook food for a family on this fire? What kind of food can be cooked in a big pot like this one?*

Assessment (R, AF2) Did the children ask relevant questions? Could they suggest answers using the text?

Objective Read and spell less common alternative graphemes including trigraphs (5.4).

(W) Find 'beautiful' on page 30. Ask children to find three letters that make the sound 'ew' as in 'flew' in this word. Practise spelling 'beautiful'. Then find 'frightened' on page 29. Ask the children to find three letters that make the sound 'i' as in 'find'. Ask them to tell you how to spell 'fright'. Think of rhyming words that have the same pattern, e.g. 'light', 'night', 'might', and make a list, asking the children to help you spell the words.

Assessment (W, AF8) Ask the children to write the following sentence from dictation: 'I might need a light at night.'

Objective Explain their reaction to texts, commenting on important aspects (8.3).

(C) (Summarising, Questioning) Ask the children to tell you briefly what happened in the story and to give reasons for their answers, e.g. ask: *Did the story take you forward or back in time? How do you know? What do you think the Viking children thought of Biff, Chip, Kipper and Wilf? What do you think they thought of the sweets? Why do you think Wilf told Biff not to leave the torch with the villagers? What would you have done?*

(C) (Imagining) Ask the children to tell you three or four things that show how life for Viking children was different from life now. Ask the children to say whether they would have liked to have visited the Vikings. Ask: *What would be good and not so good about staying in a Viking village?*

Assessment (R, AF2) Did the children use their own ideas to make inferences and deductions?

Speaking, listening and drama activities

Objective Adopt appropriate roles in small or large groups (4.1).

(C) (Imagining) Read pages 20 and 21 again. Ask children to think about the feelings of Biff, Chip, Kipper and Wilf as they waded out of the sea and the feelings of the Viking children who saw them coming.

- Ask: *Who do you think was more anxious?* Encourage them to experiment with facial expressions and gestures to show feelings.

- Ask the children to create freeze-frame moments showing: the children wading out of the sea; Kipper offering sweets to the Viking children; the Viking children tasting the sweets and after eating the sweets. What conversations might the children have? Write dialogue together and act out the scene. Allow children to change roles so that they have the opportunity to portray different characters.

Assessment *(R, AF3)* Were children able to infer how the characters felt and what they might say from the ideas in the text?

Writing activities

Objective Compose sentences using tenses consistently (present and past) (11.2).

You will need to write these sentences and each choice of verbs on the board or a large sheet of paper:
Wilf and Wilma......to the door. (come, came, coming)
Kipper......everyone about his adventure. (tells, told, telling)
The children......Mr Johnson. (like, liked, liking)
They......models of longships. (make, made, making)

- Ask the children to write the sentences, filling the gap with the word that sounds best for telling the story.

- Ask them to read their sentences aloud so that they can hear whether it sounds right.

- Ask the children to write one more sentence that tells what happened in the story.

Assessment *(W, AF6)* Did the children use the past tense consistently in their writing?

The Rainbow Machine

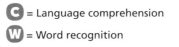

C = Language comprehension   **R, AF** = QCA reading assessment focus

W = Word recognition   **W, AF** = QCA writing assessment focus

Group or guided reading

Introducing the book

● Read the title and look briefly through the pictures to see what happens. Read the blurb on the back cover together.

C *(Clarifying)* Ask: *What is a rainbow? Can you name the colours of the rainbow? Do you think a rainbow is made by a machine? How is a rainbow made?*

C *(Prediction)* Read the blurb on the back cover. Ask: *Why do you think Nadim tries to make the machine work? What kinds of things could go wrong? Why do you think there are colours on the computer keyboard on the back page?*

Strategy check

Check that the children notice punctuation and use it to read with expression when reading aloud.

Independent reading

● Ask the children to read the story aloud. Encourage them to tackle unfamiliar words independently by using a variety of reading strategies. Praise and encourage fluent and expressive reading when children read aloud. Praise them for reading silently with concentration.

C *(Summarising)* Ask children to retell the story in just two or three sentences.

Assessment Check that children:

● *(R, AF1)* read independently and with increasing fluency longer and less familiar texts (5.1)

- (R, AF1) know how to tackle words that are not completely decodable (see the chart on page 4) (5.3)
- (R, AF1) read high and medium frequency words independently and automatically (5.5)
- (R, AF1) use syntax and context to build their store of vocabulary when reading for meaning (7.4).

Returning to the text

C (Questioning, Clarifying) Ask children to explain why Fred was left alone in charge of the Rainbow machine. Ask: *Why did he move the lorry? How did the lorry get stuck?*

C (Questioning) Ask: *Was it Fred's fault when things went wrong? Was it Nadim's fault?* Ask the children to give reasons for their opinions.

C (Summarising) Ask children to discuss the story with a partner and summarise it in no more than four sentences.

C (Clarifying) Look at page 29, ask: *Do you know what bleach is? What does it do? What do people usually use bleach for?*

Group and independent reading activities

Objective Explain their reactions to texts, commenting on important aspects (8.3).

C (Clarifying, Questioning) Ask children questions about the strange rainbows on pages 20–25: *Which rainbow do you like most? Which rainbow is a clever idea? Can you think of another strange rainbow they could have had in the story?* Ask the children to work in pairs. Ask them to choose the funniest part of the story and explain to their partner why they think it is so funny.

Assessment (R, AF2) Can the children explain their choices and reasons easily?

Objective Explore how particular words are used (7.5).

C (Questioning, Clarifying) Ask children to tell you all the question words they can think of: 'When', 'Where', 'Why', 'What', 'Who', 'How', etc. Reread page 2 and turn the statements into questions, using the question words in the list, e.g. *Where was there a lorry?, Why was it a very big lorry?.*

- Ask the children to write some questions, remembering to use question marks. Read all the questions in turn. Notice that different question words need different kinds of answers. *Which question word asks us to give a reason? Which question word needs a name for an answer? Which question word asks us to explain something? Which question word asks about the time something happened?*

Assessment *(R, AF2)* Were the children able to form questions using the most appropriate question word?

Objective Use syntax and context to build their store of vocabulary when reading for meaning (7.4).

C *(Clarifying)* Write 'What a beautiful rainbow!' on the board. Ask the children to think of some words they could use instead of 'beautiful'. Write the new sentences. Ask the children to find 'Fred turned pale' on page 27. Ask the children to think of other ways to say this. Write the new sentences. Discuss phrases that use colours to express emotions, e.g. 'He saw red', 'She turned green'.

Assessment *(R, AF2)* Could the children suggest sentences with similar meanings?

Objective Know how to tackle words that are not completely decodable (5.3).

W Find 'straight' on page 20. Ask the children to explain how they would work out this word if they did not know it. Find the phonemes that are easy to recognise (s–t–r–ai–t). Ask children to check the meaning by reading the whole sentence and looking at the illustration. On page 31, find 'fault'. Ask the children to suggest ways to read this word. Talk about using the first letter sound and the sense of the sentence to think of possible words. Prompt them to match their suggested words to the text and choose the one that makes sense and has the right letter sounds.

Assessment *(R, AF1)* Did the children have useful strategies for working out a new word?

Speaking, listening and drama activities

Objective Adopt appropriate roles in small or large groups (4.1).

- Nominate a child who reads expressively to be the narrator. Ask other children to take roles as characters in the story.

- Using pages 12–32, ask the narrator to read the narrative text, or linking sentences, and the characters to read what they say. Encourage the children to use gestures and movement to re-enact the story.

Assessment *(R, AF3)* Can children say each character's dialogue in the appropriate tone of voice?

Writing activities

Objective Draw on knowledge of texts in deciding and planning what and how to write (9.1).

C *(Imagining)* Discuss how the rainbow machine went wrong and what was funny in the story. Think of ideas for other imaginary weather machines. Make a list, then think about how the machines might work. Ask: *How might a snow machine work? Or a mobile freezing unit for ice skating? Or a sunshine machine for cloudy days?*

- Ask the children to describe the kind of machine it is, how it works, what it does and what goes wrong with it. They will need to decide how it is put right and how the story will end. They could write a sequence of sentences as a plan first. They will also need to decide upon a title.

- Make time for children to write their stories.

Assessment *(R, AF1)* Can children write an imaginative story plan, then write the story?

The Flying Carpet

The Flying Carpet

> **C** = Language comprehension **R, AF** = QCA reading assessment focus
>
> **W** = Word recognition **W, AF** = QCA writing assessment focus

Group or guided reading

Introducing the book

● Read the title and talk about the picture on the cover. Look briefly through the pictures to see what happens.

C *(Clarifying)* Ask: *Where do you think the story takes place? How can you tell? Do you know any other stories about flying carpets? Do you know how a flying carpet works?*

C *(Prediction)* Read the blurb on the back cover. Ask: *Do you think the boy in the picture is in this country or another country? What makes you think that? What do you think will happen in this story?*

Strategy check

Check that the children use a variety of strategies to make sense of the text.

Independent reading

● Ask the children to read the story. Remind them to use phonics and the sense of the sentence to work out new words. Praise children for reading silently with concentration, and for reading aloud with expression.

C *(Summarising)* Ask children to tell you quickly what the story was about and what they liked about it.

Assessment Check that children:

● *(R, AF1)* read independently and with increasing fluency longer and less familiar texts (5.1)

● *(R, AF1)* know how to tackle words that are not completely decodable (see chart on page 4) (5.3)

(R, AF1) read high and medium frequency words independently and automatically (5.5)

- (R, AF1) use syntax and context to build their store of vocabulary when reading for meaning (7.4).

Returning to the text

C (*Summarising*) Ask the children to explain who was rescued and why. Ask: *Why was the uncle wicked?*

C (*Questioning*) Look at pages 16–19. Ask: *Why are these pictures in thought clouds? Who is telling this part of the story? When did these events happen?* Introduce the term 'flashback' to name the technique for recounting past events in a story.

C (*Imagining*) Ask: *Where does this story take place? Can you find any words that describe the landscape?* ('deserts' and 'mountains' on page 10). Ask the children to close their eyes and imagine this setting. Ask: *What can you see? What can you hear?*

Group and independent reading activities

Objective Draw together ideas and information from across a whole text, using simple signposts in the text (7.1).

C (*Clarifying/Prediction*) Ask the children to decide who they think is the 'bad' character in this story. Find descriptions of the boy's uncle on pages 15–18. Make a list of the words that describe his character. Ask: *What happens to this character at the end of the story? How can you tell that the boy was a nicer character?* Find evidence on page 16 and pages 24–26.

Assessment (R, AF2) Can the children find evidence in the text to support their ideas of the characters?

Objective Read independently and with increasing fluency longer and less familiar texts (5.1).

W Ask the children to read a section of the story to you. Ask questions about this part of the story. Ask them to explain how they worked out any unfamiliar words. Turn to page 27. Ask them to explain the purpose of the ellipsis in the last sentence: 'I wonder if…?'.

Assessment *(R, AF1)* Did the children read independently with confidence and fluency? Could they explain the ellipsis?

Objective Use syntax and context to build their store of vocabulary when reading for meaning (7.4).

Ⓒ *(Clarifying)* Read page 19 again. Ask the children to read the last sentence aloud. Ask: *What is a hostage?* Use the context on this page to work out why it helps the uncle to keep the boy in prison. On page 21, find the word 'zoomed'. Ask: *Is this a better word to use than 'flew' or 'went'? Can you explain why?* On page 26, find the word 'punished'. Ask: *What does this word mean?* Ask the children to think of other words to use instead, e.g. 'imprisoned', 'taught a lesson', 'locked up'.

Assessment *(R, AF3)* Can the children work out the meaning of the word 'hostage'? Could they suggest synonyms and say why one word sounds better than another?

Objective Spell with increasing accuracy and confidence, drawing on word recognition and knowledge of word structure, and spelling patterns (5.2).

Ⓦ Ask the children to look at page 15 and find a word that ends with '-ly'. Ask: *Can you think of another word that ends with '-ly' that means the same thing?* (e.g. 'unhappily', 'miserably'). Make a list of '-ly' words. Notice whether the base word changes when '-ly' is added: for example, words that do not change include 'sadly', 'quickly', 'kindly', 'suddenly'; words in which 'y' becomes 'i' are 'happily', 'speedily', 'steadily'; words in which the final 'e' is dropped include 'miserably', 'sensibly', 'horribly'.

Assessment *(R, AF1)* Can children identify the '-ly' suffix in words and think of other words with the same suffix?

Speaking, listening and drama activities

Objective Present part of stories for members of their own class (4.2).

You will need card, felt pens, sellotape, lollypop sticks and pieces of fabric.

 (Imagining) Discuss putting on a puppet show to tell the boy's story from pages 16–19. Ask the children to think of a title, e.g. 'The Wicked Uncle Kidnaps the King'. Make a list of characters you will need and make stick puppets for them. Ask children to choose characters, paint faces and attach them to sticks, then drape fabric over the sticks for costumes.

● Ask the children to discuss what the characters will say and the types of voices they will use.

● Encourage them to act out the play with enthusiasm.

Assessment *(R, AF3)* Have children interpreted their characters' words using the correct tone of voice?

Writing activities

Objective Explain their reactions to texts, commenting on important aspects (8.3).

● Ask the children, in pairs, to say what they liked about this story. Ask them to write a letter to their partner telling them why this is a good story to read. They could cover the main points by completing these sentences:
The story is about…
It is exciting when…
It is funny when…
The character I liked best was…because…

● Discuss ways of mentioning the ending without giving it all away. Write the suggestions on the board, e.g. 'The children finally outwit the wicked uncle.' 'After an exciting adventure the boy becomes king again.'

Assessment *(W, AF3)* Can the children structure a letter, presenting their ideas about the story clearly and logically?

A Day in London

> **C** = Language comprehension   **R, AF** = QCA reading assessment focus
>
> **W** = Word recognition   **W, AF** = QCA writing assessment focus

Group or guided reading

Introducing the book

- Read the title, talk about the cover picture and read the blurb on the back. Briefly look through the pictures to see what happens.

- **C** *(Clarifying)* Ask: *Have you been to London? What famous places did you see? Did you visit any parks or museums?*

- **C** *(Prediction)* Ask the children to say what they think will happen in the story. *Is it a magic adventure? What do you think it might mean when it says that 'Things don't go quite as Gran planned'?*

Strategy check

Remind the children to reread a sentence if it doesn't seem to make sense.

Independent reading

- Ask the children to read the story. Remind them to use phonics and the sense of the sentence to work out new words. Praise children for reading silently with concentration, and for reading aloud with expression.

- **C** *(Summarising)* Ask children to tell you the main point of the story. *What, exactly, didn't go as Gran planned?*

Assessment Check that children:

- *(R, AF1)* read independently and with increasing fluency longer and less familiar texts (5.1)

- *(R, AF1)* know how to tackle words that are not completely decodable (see chart on page 4) (5.3)

- *(R, AF1)* read high and medium frequency words independently and automatically (5.5)

● (R, AF1) use syntax and context to build their store of vocabulary when reading for meaning (7.4).

Returning to the text

C (Questioning) Ask: *Who did Gran take to London? How did they get there? Why did Mum say that Gran was worse than the children?* Look at page 9. Ask: *Why did Mum ask Biff to look after Gran? What would you expect Mum to say?*

C (Clarifying) Ask: *What did Gran do in the waxworks? Did the attendant think Gran was funny?*

W Go back to page 12. Find 'Trafalgar'. Ask the children to show you how to break this word down into syllables (Tra–fal–gar).

Group and independent reading activities

Objective Draw together ideas and information from across a text (7.1).

C (Questioning) Look at page 8. Ask: *Do you think Gran knows where she is going? What is Dad doing?* Look at page 9. *What has happened to Biff? Have you seen this happen in another story?* Look at pages 31 and 32. Ask: *What other adventure did the children and Gran have on the way home? How do you know? What do you think was the problem with the car? What will Mum and Dad say? What is about to happen to the man with the dog on page 30?*

Assessment (R, AF3) Could the children use information from the illustrations to describe the journey home? Can they suggest what Mum and Dad might have said?

Objective Explore how particular words are used (7.5).

C (Questioning, Clarifying) Look at page 11. Ask: *What does Anneena say about the tube? Why is it funny?* Look at page 14. *Why is it funny to say that the Queen must be busy cleaning rooms?* Look at page 32. *What does the word 'beheading' mean? What did Gran mean about beheading the Queen?*

Assessment (R, AF3) Can children explain the humour in the way these words are used?

Objective Use syntax and context to build their store of vocabulary when reading for meaning (7.4).

C (*Questioning*) Ask the children to find the question on page 3. *What did Kipper want to know? Can they find the answer in the story?* Then ask them to find the question on page 7. *Does Dad want to find something out, or is he just wondering?* On pages 18 and 19, Kipper asks two questions. Which question is trying to find something out? On page 20, what does Kipper want to know? On page 24, find a question where Biff is wondering about something.

● Ask the children to make up a question to find out information, using 'What', 'When', 'Who', or 'Where'. Then ask them to think of a question to find out a reason about something, using a 'Why' question. Talk about different types of questions.

Assessment (R, AF3) Can the children suggest different types of questions?

Objective Know how to tackle unfamiliar words (5.3).

W Ask the children to look for the longest words they can find in the story. Make a list, e.g. 'Victoria', 'Trafalgar', 'grandchildren', 'boomerangs', 'squeezed'. Say each word in turn and clap the syllables. Write the word in syllables (Vic–tor–i–a). Ask: *Which word has only one syllable? Which ways could help you remember how to spell 'squeezed'?*

● Think of words with 'qu' at the beginning, e.g. 'question', 'quarter', 'quiet', 'quarrel', 'queue'. Look at each word in turn and, together, think of ways to help remember how to spell them, e.g. say: *'queue' has 'u' and 'e' queueing up in turn.*

Assessment (R, AF8) Can the children use syllables to read and spell the words?

Speaking, listening and drama activities

Objective Adopt appropriate roles in small or large groups (4.1).

C (*Imagining*) Ask children to volunteer to be in the hot seat as Gran, Biff, Chip, Kipper, Anneena and Nadim. Ask the class to think of questions to ask them about their day in London and questions such as: *Why did you come back on a breakdown lorry? What do you not* *want Mum and Dad to know?* Ask the characters to answer in role, using information from the story and additional ideas from their imagination.

Writing activities

Objective Draw on knowledge and experience of texts in deciding and planning what and how to write (9.1).

You will need pictures of famous places in London from the story, from information books or the Internet.

- Talk about the places in London that the children and Gran visited in order. Make a list. Show the pictures of famous places in London. Which places would the children like to visit?

- Ask the children to work with a partner and plan a day in London. They can then use their plans to describe their day out to the rest of the class.

Assessment *(R, AF1)* Could the children use the structure of this story to plan a day in London for themselves?

Victorian Adventure

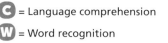

C = Language comprehension		*R, AF* = QCA reading assessment focus	
W = Word recognition		*W, AF* = QCA writing assessment focus	

Group or guided reading

Introducing the book

- Read the title, look at the picture and read the blurb on the back cover. Have a quick look through the pages of the book to see what happens.

C *(Prediction)* Ask: *What do you think the surprise at Buckingham Palace might be?*

C *(Clarifying)* Ask: *Who can explain what 'Victorian' means? Do you know how long ago Queen Victoria lived?* (1837–1901).

C *(Questioning)* Ask: *How can you tell that this story is set in the past?* Ask the children to look at the pages that give clues and say what the clues are, e.g. pages 8, 9 and 10.

Strategy check

Remind children to use their knowledge of phonics to work out new words.

Independent reading

- Ask the children to read the story. Remind them to use phonics and the sense of the sentence to work out new words. Praise children for reading silently with concentration, and for reading aloud with expression.

Assessment Check that children:

- *(R, AF1)* read independently and with increasing fluency longer and less familiar texts (5.1)

- *(R, AF1)* know how to tackle words that are not completely decodable (see chart on page 4) (5.3)

- (R, AF1) read high and medium frequency words independently and automatically (5.5)
- (R, AF1) use syntax and context to build their store of vocabulary when reading for meaning (7.4).

Returning to the text

🅒 *(Questioning)* On page 6, ask: *How does the text on this page tell us the time when the story was set?*

🅒 *(Questioning)* On page 13, ask: *How did Biff know where they were? Does this mean that the palace has changed or stayed the same?*

🅒 *(Clarifying)* Turn to page 27. *Why did Kipper think that they might have their heads chopped off?*

🅒 *(Questioning)* Ask: *What was the surprise at Buckingham Palace that is mentioned on the back cover?*

Group and independent reading activities

Objective Give some reasons why things happen (7.2).

🅒 *(Questioning)* Look at page 4. Ask: *Why do you think the magic took them to Victorian London?* Look back at pages 2 and 3. *What have you noticed about the way the magic works?* Page 8: *Why did Vicky take the children to see the blacksmith?* Find and read the answer on page 7. Page 14: *Why was there a flashing light from the palace?* Find the answer suggested on the same page and the evidence in the picture on page 16. Page 24: *Why were the children taken to prison?* Find the reasons on page 23. *Why was Biff worried?* Find the answer on page 24. Page 28: *Why do you think Gran and Queen Victoria liked each other?* Praise children for using their own ideas and knowledge of Gran to answer this question.

Assessment (R, AF2) Were the children able to give reasons for the events in the story? Where appropriate, could they find the evidence in the text?

Objective Draw together ideas and information from across a whole text, using simple signposts in the text (7.1).

🅒 *(Clarifying)* Use the text and pictures on pages 10 and 11, then on pages 18 and 19, to find clues that show the story is set in the past. Make two lists headed 'Pictures' and 'Words'. List the objects in the pictures, e.g. pump, Vicky's clothes, and words and phrases from the text, e.g. 'Vicky pumped the water…', 'She bought some bread with the penny'. Find more clues on other pages. Record the page number where children discover the text next to the words in the lists.

Assessment *(R, AF2)* Can children find clues to the setting throughout the story? Can they locate the evidence?

Objective Explain their reaction to texts, commenting on important aspects (8.3).

C *(Summarising)* Ask children to choose another Oxford Reading Tree book at Stage 8 and compare it with *Victorian Adventure*. Summarise both stories in three or four sentences. You could use the story summary from the notes on the inside cover of one of the books as an example. Ask the children to say which story they prefer and why.

Assessment *(R, AF2)* Were the children able to use main points from the stories to make comparisons? Did they give reasons for their opinions?

Objective Spell with increasing accuracy and confidence, drawing on word recognition and knowledge of structure, and spelling patterns (5.2).

W Ask the children, in pairs, to look through the story for one-, two-, three- and four-syllable words, then to write at least two words for each type. (You may need to match the instructions to the ability of the children. Some children may only manage one- and two-syllable words. More able children could be asked to choose words with five letters or more.) Ask children to break each word down into syllables (e.g. im–por–tant) and then help each other learn the spellings, before testing each other.

Assessment *(R, AF1)* Ask the children to tell the group a word on their list and then to spell it. Could the children spell the words accurately?

Speaking, listening and drama activities

Objective Explain ideas using imaginative and expressive vocabulary (1.3).

C *(Imagining)* Look at the pictures of Victorian children in the story, then ask the children to imagine that a Victorian child has arrived in their class today. Ask them to close their eyes and picture the child.

Ask one or two children to describe the child they have imagined. Invite a volunteer to be in the hot seat as the Victorian child and ask the class to think of questions to ask him/her.

Writing activities

Objective Draw on knowledge and experience of texts in deciding and planning what and how to write (9.1).

C *(Imagining)* Ask the children to discuss Gran's adventure with a partner. Prompt them to think of these questions: *Where was Gran when the key glowed? How did she get to Buckingham Palace? How did she meet Queen Victoria? Did the servants find her first? What did Gran say to them? Why did Gran and Queen Victoria have plenty to talk about?*

● Ask the children to make notes of their ideas as a plan, then begin writing 'Gran's Victorian Adventure'.

Assessment *(W, AF3)* Could the children invent events that led up to Gran meeting Queen Victoria? *(W, AF2)* Could they write the story?

Oxford Reading Tree resources at this level

Biff, Chip and Kipper
Stage 8 Stories
Stage 8 More Stories A

Poetry
Glow-worms Stage 8–9

Non-fiction
Stage 8 Fireflies

Wider reading
Stage 8 Snapdragons

Electronic
Stage 8–9 Talking Stories
e-Songbirds
e-Fireflies
MagicPage
Clip Art
ORT Online www.OxfordReadingTree.com

Teachers' Resources
Comprehension Photocopy Masters
(Stages 6–9)
Context Cards
Teacher's Handbook (Stages 1–9)
Group Activity Sheets
Phonics and Spelling Activities (Stages 1–9)
Stage 8 Workbooks
Songbirds Teaching Notes, Guided Reading
Cards and Parent Notes
Fireflies Teaching Notes, Guided Reading
Cards and Take Home Cards

OXFORD
UNIVERSITY PRESS

Great Clarendon Street, Oxford OX2 6DP

Oxford University Press is a department of the University of
Oxford. It furthers the University's objective of excellence in
research, scholarship, and education by publishing worldwide in

Oxford   New York

Auckland   Cape Town   Dar es Salaam   Hong Kong   Karachi
Kuala Lumpur   Madrid   Melbourne   Mexico City   Nairobi
New Delhi   Shanghai   Taipei   Toronto

With offices in

Argentina   Austria   Brazil   Chile   Czech Republic   France
Greece   Guatemala   Hungary   Italy   Japan   Poland
Portugal   Singapore   South Korea   Switzerland
Thailand   Turkey   Ukraine   Vietnam

Oxford is a registered trade mark of Oxford University Press
in the UK and in certain other countries

Text © Oxford University Press 2008

Written by Thelma Page, based on the orginal characters created
by Roderick Hunt and Alex Brychta.

The moral rights of the author have been asserted

Database right Oxford University Press (maker)

First published 2008

British Library Cataloguing in Publication Data

Data available

Cover illustrations Alex Brychta

ISBN: 978-0-19-846612-3

10 9 8 7 6 5

Page make-up by Thomson Digital

Printed in China by Imago

Paper used in the production of this book is a natural, recyclable
product made from wood grown in sustainable forests. The
manufacturing process conforms to the environmental
regulations of the country of origin.